W9-ACR-380

Baby Orangutans

by Christina Leaf

BELLWETHER MEDIA • MINNEAPOLIS, MN

Note to Librarians, Teachers, and Parents:

Blastoff! Readers are carefully developed by literacy experts and combine standards-based content with developmentally appropriate text.

Level 1 provides the most support through repetition of high-frequency words, light text, predictable sentence patterns, and strong visual support.

Level 2 offers early readers a bit more challenge through varied simple sentences, increased text load, and less repetition of high-frequency words.

Level 3 advances early-fluent readers toward fluency through increased text and concept load, less reliance on visuals, longer sentences, and more literary language.

Level 4 builds reading stamina by providing more text per page, increased use of punctuation, greater variation in sentence patterns, and increasingly challenging vocabulary.

Level 5 encourages children to move from "learning to read" to "reading to learn" by providing even more text, varied writing styles, and less familiar topics.

Whichever book is right for your reader, Blastoff! Readers are the perfect books to build confidence and encourage a love of reading that will last a lifetime!

This edition first published in 2015 by Bellwether Media, Inc.

No part of this publication may be reproduced in whole or in part without written permission of the publisher. For information regarding permission, write to Bellwether Media, Inc., Attention: Permissions Department, 5357 Penn Avenue South, Minneapolis, MN 55419.

Library of Congress Cataloging-in-Publication Data

Leaf, Christina, author.
  Baby Orangutans / by Christina Leaf.
    pages cm. – (Blastoff! Readers. Super Cute!)
  Summary: "Developed by literacy experts for students in kindergarten through grade three, this book introduces baby orangutans to young readers through leveled text and related photos."– Provided by publisher.
  Audience: Ages 5-8.
  Audience: K to grade 3.
  Includes bibliographical references and index.
  ISBN 978-1-62617-171-8 (hardcover : alk. paper)
  1. Orangutans–Infancy–Juvenile literature. I. Title. II. Series: Blastoff! Readers. 1, Super Cute!
  QL737.P94L43 2015
  599.88'313'92–dc23
                        2014034759

Printed in the United States of America, North Mankato, MN.

Table of Contents

Orangutan Infant!

A baby orangutan is called an infant. It lives in the **rain forest**.

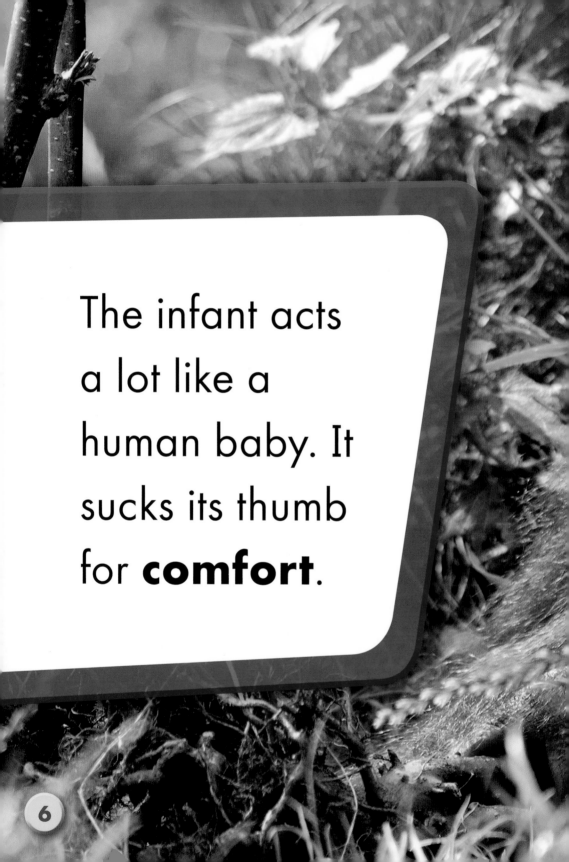

The infant acts a lot like a human baby. It sucks its thumb for **comfort**.

Life With Mom

The baby **clings** to mom's belly as a **newborn**. Mom carries it through the trees.

The baby needs to grow strong. It drinks mom's milk for food.

Mom **grooms** the baby. She picks dirt and bugs out of its hair.

The pair shares a tight **bond** for about six years.

Learning From Mom

Mom teaches the infant to live in the trees. She shows how to build a nest to sleep in.

They find food together. Mom knows where to get tasty fruits.

The baby also learns to climb. It swings from trees and **vines**. Whee!

Glossary

bond—a close connection

clings—hangs on tight and close

comfort—a feeling of peace

grooms—cleans

newborn—a baby that was just recently born

rain forest—a warm forest that receives a lot of rain

vines—plants that twist up trees; some vines hang from tree branches.

To Learn More

AT THE LIBRARY

Borgert-Spaniol, Megan. *Orangutans*. Minneapolis, Minn.: Bellwether Media, 2014.

Eszterhas, Suzi. *Orangutan*. London, U.K.: Frances Lincoln Children's Books, 2013.

Leaf, Christina. *Baby Gorillas*. Minneapolis, Minn.: Bellwether Media, 2015.

ON THE WEB

Learning more about orangutans is as easy as 1, 2, 3.

1. Go to www.factsurfer.com.

2. Enter "orangutans" into the search box.

3. Click the "Surf" button and you will see a list of related web sites.

With factsurfer.com, finding more information is just a click away.

Index